AFTER METROPOLIS

THE ARCHITECTURE & DESIGN OF POWELL TUCK ASSOCIATES

JULIAN POWELL-TUCK

Artifice
books on architecture

To my wife Dinah and our children Jonah, Freddie, Maudie and Tabby

CONTENTS

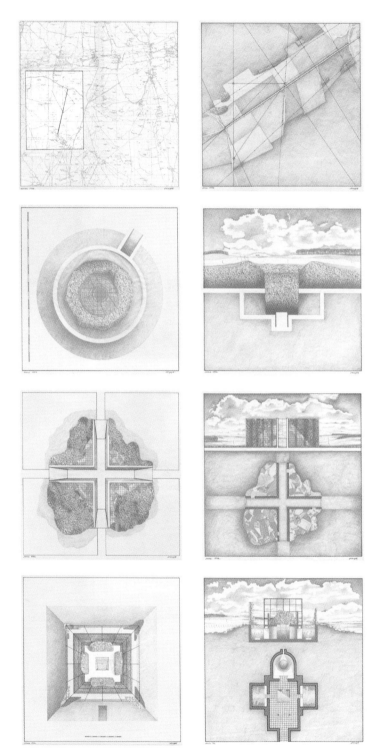

3 HOUSES IN A LANDSCAPE 1976
JULIAN POWELL-TUCK

CROSSING BOUNDARIES

I blame Hugh Casson. If it weren't for his fabulously inclusive course on design at The Royal College of Art in London, I would not have been such a mixed up kid. There were students and tutors from all disciplines and we studied themes around Architecture, Landscape, Interiors, Furniture for a postgraduate course called "Environmental Design".

In the 1970s this did not mean what it does today. It was simply about designing our environment through proposals of differing scales. It allowed our interests to move between the traditional disciplines of Architecture, Landscape and Interior Design. Since then I have always struggled to define what I do. This has sometimes presented its problems... however it provided the confidence to cross boundaries and was to become the design philosophy of Powell Tuck Associates.

At the RCA I became interested less in 'built form' itself, than in how 'built form' was occupied. I was concerned with the space between forms, enjoying the freedom of designing a landscape or an interior as much as a building itself. My final project at the RCA was about three megalithic houses in a landscape, which were temporally ambiguous pieces of modern architecture that had been archeologically re-discovered. Ever since, when someone asks whether one of our designs is new build or existing, or says it's as though it has been there for years, I take it as a sign that it has gone in the right direction.

We choose materials that might have local significance, not to fit in, but rather to have this temporal ambiguity... is it old or is it new? It's a philosophy borne out of enjoying altering buildings. It has always seemed to me that the art of altering an existing building is as engaging and challenging as that of building new. As working with existing buildings is such a large part of the architectural metier in the UK, I am surprised that it is not taken more seriously in architectural schools. Maybe this is the reason why building conversions are often done so badly. Personally I find alternative strategies for altering buildings fascinating and, if more people did, perhaps we might end up with a better building stock.

During the 1980s I taught in the school of 3D Design at Kingston University where our particular focus was the rehabilitation and re-use of existing buildings. During this fascinating period both staff and students enjoyed exploring strategies for altering buildings, and, with Fred Scott, I worked on a definition of these strategies. They were exciting times. We felt that we were adding conceptual meat to the study of Interior Design, so often dismissed as ephemeral and lightweight in wider architectural circles.

In simple terms our philosophy for altering buildings went like this.
We need to understand the following in the alteration of existing buildings:

- How the building worked and functioned when it was originally conceived
- How the building could or should be reduced or 'stripped back' prior to taking change
- The extent and form of re-modelling that a building needs for re-use
- The choice of architectural language for the new works.

These components, in my opinion, are the essence of a successful building alteration. By treating existing buildings in this way one adopts a super-sensitivity to the context in which one builds. The list fails to tackle how a building should function for a new use. Is it the role of the designer to provide a well-conceived setting for the pre-established way in which a building should work, or should the designer challenge these pre-conceptions and suggest new ways of occupation? Just as we need to develop a super-sensitivity to our physical environment, we needed to undertake a similar level of scrutiny of how people use, or behave within, spaces.

Product designers are good at this. They prototype a product and let people test it, use it, react to it, before it is finally put on the market. People, now used to this, have high expectations of new design. However it's a dangerous business trying to change the way in which occupants are expected to use a building. A new building is only a prototype and, if an architect is expected to get it right in one go, it is hardly surprising a cautious approach is often adopted.

I have always felt that we shouldn't attempt to make futuristic architecture: we should just produce architecture that responds to the world as it exists now. Designers need to respond to the way people use or could use a building. Observing how people occupy buildings should be a favourite pastime of every budding designer.

These general strategies, born out of the study of altering architecture, have been the backbone of the practice for over 20 years. Like all strategies they become flexible over time. They are of course equally relevant to building new as for refurbishment. They do not cover the art of creating a well-proportioned space, selecting an appropriate material, or the use of light, all of which are key central concerns in the practice. Both theory and practice merge over time.

Whilst working on my final year project "3 houses in a Landscape" as a postgraduate student at the RCA, the new professor of Architecture, John Miller, called me into his study for a chat. He was struggling to understand what my project was about. I explained it was about man's initial response to landscape. How I imagined landing on an undeveloped landscape and responding... I was exploring notions of measurement, landmark, orientation, geological and historical layers, all in an attempt to define a direction for my new architecture.

He looked baffled and said that in his mind architecture was simply about "quality of life". Well 'quality of life' for me at that stage of my life centred on getting drunk, getting laid and financially getting by, so it was my turn to look baffled and I asked for an explanation. He replied that for him it meant the simple things in life, like getting up in the morning, "sitting out on a balcony with a great view and drinking a good cup of coffee".

I was dumb-found: surely architectural theory could not be that simple. Now nearly 40 years on as I walk onto my balcony at Sentry with my morning cup of coffee, I remember this session... maybe he had a point.

I founded Powell Tuck Associates in 1990 out of my previous practice Powell Tuck Connor and Orefelt (PTCO). My team within PTCO joined me in the new venture and, of that team, Angus Shepherd and Adrian Lees have worked with me continuously since then. They are now running the show.

This book celebrates the early years of the practice. From the early 1990s work, that was more visually expressive as it attempted to express theoretical notions, to the later calmer work, which strangely seems to have come full circle and express notions first explored whilst still a student. We have not tried to choose our 'greatest hits' but rather projects that mean a lot to us and represent key stages in the development of the practice. The descriptions of these projects will be personal, somewhat quirky, and very much from an angle. They will not give all the facts and figures and will certainly omit copious credits due to clients, contractors, and design teams who have worked on them with us.

JULIAN POWELL-TUCK

METROPOLIS STUDIOS

METROPOLIS STUDIOS
1986–1990

One of the joys of being a designer is that you gain knowledge not only about construction, but also about the use of the building which you have designed. Strangely, in the early years of the practice there was more chance of a commission for which you had no direct experience. In those days there seemed to be more owner/entrepreneurs who were the key decision-makers. One such person was Carey Taylor who, after years as a sound engineer, had a calling to build a new state of the art recording studio. With a small group of co-investors he found a possible space for the studio in West London and, guided by both an acoustician and a project manager, invited a group of architects to submit initial designs for its conversion. Experience of designing studios was not a prerequisite, but the practice had recently completed some post-production video facilities in Camden and did have some experience of highly technical fit-out work.

The chosen space was a part of an enormous power station built originally in 1901 to power the first stretch of tramway in West London. It was designed by a young William Curtis Green. The tramway was only viable for a few years and the buildings soon became redundant. The outer sheds eventually were re-developed as a bus station, and the main power house fell into disrepair. The boilers and turbines were removed and all that remained was a leaking building envelope and two fine West and South facades. In 1984 a property developer, having obtained planning permission for a mixed development of 19 apartments, office space, a film studio, and car parking, converted the building. The envelope was restored and a large concrete floor slab was installed at high level to support the apartments. The main turbine hall was split in two by a vast cross-wall, separating the office development from the studio space.

Having won the competition, there then followed a feasibility period during which we explored design strategies for the building works, and how the available budget could be made to set the project in motion. Finally we settled on a phased strategy that built the structure for the complex and initially

only fitted out the two biggest studios, leaving further development for later phases. The original project managers and acoustician had by now left the process and PTA was appointed to head up a traditional design team. Sam Toyoshima was appointed acoustician consultant along with his associate in the UK, John Flynn.

In spite of the enormous proportions of the shell space our proposals were a tight fit from the outset, particularly in the height dimension. If recording studios are stacked and have residential units above, many layers of acoustic isolation are needed. Housing the air handling plant was a particular challenge, as the roof space had been used for apartments. The building's listed building status meant that every alteration had to be negotiated with the planners. We came up with the notion of a sandwich structure, with studios being the outer layers and the plant, cafe, bar and recreational areas the filling. This way the studio layers were separated to allow the required acoustic isolation and service space. The new structure was held away from the original tiled elevation so that we could maximise the use of daylight available from the two huge west-facing windows and retain the sense of drama and scale of the original turbine hall.

The accepted wisdom from conservationists is that when you are fitting out listed buildings the new works should only engage minimally with the envelope and should be lightweight, presumably so that all can be cleared away again at a later date, without affecting the original design. This strategy assumes that the new

design will be inferior to the original and certainly would not have struck a chord with Robert Adam when he remodeled Syon House. The lightweight approach did not work for us, mainly because we needed mass for acoustic isolation between the studios, and we rather liked the idea of giving the new use a confident permanence that would withstand the rough treatment of the 'rock and roll' industry.

I wanted to introduce temporal ambiguity to the design, where the new structure felt permanent and there was an expressed movement between the old and new works, allowing each to be both distinguished and clearly distinguishable. The existing floor of the turbine was excavated and the new works founded on an existing deep concrete slab. This had been built originally to support the large turbines and was decoupled from the architectural shell structure. It provided a perfect foundation for the new studios. The new structure was to rise out of the basement and was conceived to be passing through the original building, like a great liner waiting at the quayside. The design detail of the access stairs, platforms and equipment lift to studios express this notion of the decoupling of the two structures.

Conceptually there were three layers to the design: 1) the building envelope, the structure inherited after its first conversion, 2) the new support structure and interior architecture, which primarily dealt with sound isolation between the studios and, 3) the studio fit-out, which gave each studio its particular acoustic treatment. There was

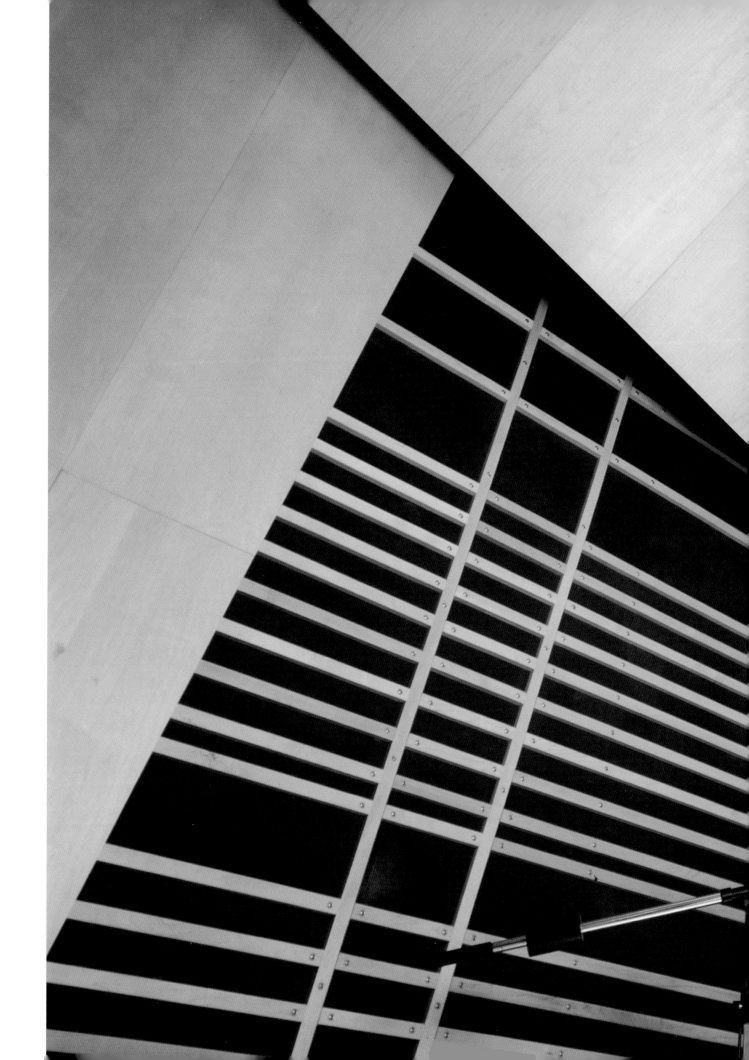

much debate about the finish of the new internal facade. Rendered block-work seemed the obvious choice to everyone but us. We wanted something more permanent that would age well and take the knocks. We settled on concrete with a stone aggregate of a similar hue to the green glazed tiles in the original building. The wall was poured on site and then scabbled back by power tools to reveal the green aggregate. With hindsight this was a great decision supported by a visionary client. The vast studio elevation looks as good now, 25 years later, as it did when it was built, and has needed no decoration or maintenance.

I was later told we got the job because we produced an architectural concept that would allow the studios to be the particular complex shapes they needed to be to sound right. In the 1980s Recording Studios were beginning to be used differently as more and more of the process was taking place in the control room rather that the studio space itself. The big idea at Metropolis was to make the control room the focus of each studio, rather than a technical room tacked onto a studio, which was the historical precedent. Control rooms now needed to become bigger and be able to accommodate both engineers and musicians and their gear.

Studio A was originally designed to house a vast curved mixing console. Tall acoustically tuned studios were wrapped around the control room. Associated private recreational accommodation for the bands looked onto the studio from above the control room. The studio linings were designed to accommodate acoustic trapping, lighting and ventilation and were sculpted to enhance the room's acoustics. Each studio was glazed to the atrium to claim a share of the daylight given from the two main atrium windows. I have always liked to believe that there was some link between the quality of sound in the studios and the quality of the architectural space... but I am not sure scientists would necessarily agree! However the associated knowledge gained through our work on recording studios has been invaluable.

The first five studios we designed were all drawn with pen and ink on drawing boards, as this was before design went digital. Up until then studio fit-outs had traditionally been carried out by specialist studio fit-out contractors. They produced few detailed drawings, as the design was a closely guarded secret. At Metropolis we drew all the construction detail and the studios were constructed by non-specialist, highly-competent, fit-out contractors. This was some feat.

PTA worked on the studios as the development expanded to include five studios and further mastering rooms, programming and editing suites. We also went on to design associated mastering rooms in New York.

METROPOLIS STUDIOS

LAMPTON PLACE
1995–1996

This small-scale project is included because for us it demonstrates some of the ideas about building alteration that were around at that time. The building that was to take the new use didn't need to be a masterpiece to deserve respect. Our initial thought was to make the existing building whole again, so that it could hold its ground against the changes that were to be made.

We made it structurally sound, restored the brickwork and the roof. A vast new garage door was made to re-hang from the original door track. Walls were insulated and lined, and new floor slab installed. The building, in a London mews, was originally designed to house a coach and horses, the mode of transport for a neighbouring household. It was the one building in the mews that hadn't been 'altered'. At that time this meant made to look like a twee small house or cottage.

The idea was simply to reinforce the original building so that the memory of its former use could remain. A new upper floor was added with a new glazed facade inserted just inside the huge single opening in the facade. This new facade was specified to modern standards of insulation and security. A stair was introduced between the original facade and a new glazed one. The double elevation allowed us to solve means of escape from the upper studio space and neatly hide new services and an air-handling system in the space between. It left the remaining workspaces spacious and uncluttered.

The client was a toy designer renowned for designing the children toy hit of the time "Polly Pockets". New products were created within this building. They particularly liked the way the building would shut down out of hours, but with the door open would become animated and active at work.

M SALON
1994

This is another fit-out project from PTA early years, but this time the 'host' was neither 'Listed' nor an interesting building type. Instead it was a newly finished retail unit in an office development sited at the junction of Avery Row and Grosvenor Street in Mayfair, London. The developers expected that the retail shell provided would be hidden behind the new fit-out works, but we felt that, left uncovered, both the moodiness and patina of the rough concrete and scale of the lofty existing space would add drama and interest to the proposal. We were to insert newly defined elements to transform it. At the time this approach was labelled as "interventionist", though we prefer the term "contextural'. We were working with a heightened regard for context, not necessarily the quality of the space in strict architectural terms, but rather how its intrinsic nature could be used to enrich a proposal.

The block-work walls, concrete ceiling and a new sand and cement screed floor became the perfect backdrop for a series of key elements, somewhere between joinery and fit-out, that provided the functional requirements. Galvanised metal stair treads, screened behind a vivid lime green blade, led to the upper office, store and staff area. Ceiling planes that contain lighting and services, appear as though they are cut out of the new partitions. Cutting stations are simply defined each with its own vast mirror and a grey storage box. Hinged mirrors in the tall bay window provide both screening from, and display to, the street. A reception desk is set in a commanding position by the entrance door and includes a simple display unit and a coat-hanging structure behind. A tiled hair washing space is sited at a more intimate scale under the mezzanine floor.

The space was the first hair and makeup salon for the international stylist, Michio Fukuda, and was soon followed by another in Tokyo, also designed by PTA.

M SALON

M SALON

THE BIRMINGHAM BOYS

I met Julian when I started teaching in Hugh Casson's School of Environmental Design at the Royal College of Art in the mid 70s. It was Sir Hugh's last year of running this the School he had founded, before his retirement. His style of management was to have all the tutors meet together at 10.00 am on Mondays for a casual mulling over of the students, their work and their progress or otherwise. Useful gossip could be exchanged at these gatherings, the atmosphere being conducive to this. After that we were left to get on with it. We were on the sixth floor, at the top (was it?) on the East end of the Darwin block. The startling proximity of the roof of the Albert Hall out the windows was familiar to me. The grand Victorian terrace that had previously stood on the site had been given over for student's to live in prior to its demolition. I had lived there, during my first summer in London. The roof was flat, and we could walk its length, astride the city, and drop down into other houses. It was the scorching summer of 1959; John Furnival sat up there day after day with a bottle of ink and a pen drawing a full panorama of South Kensington and the Park, including the bottle of ink.

One day in the RCA Junior Common Rooms, on the first floor, which was previously and occasionally a ballroom, in the grand house in Cromwell Road on the corner of Cromwell Place, the architect Cadbury Brown explained to us assembled munching art students the new buildings to be built in Kensington Gore after I had graduated. We pretended indifference, but I remember his concern for the front building on the road forming a composition with the Albert Hall and Norman Shaw's mansion block beyond, and his explaining the short section, the interlocking pattern of tall and not so tall spaces that has served and continues to serve the purposes of the College so well.

When completed the Kensington Gore block had at the back, south-facing at the top, a double-height greenhouse. It intercepted one of the top routes along the building and took it on a bridge through the jungle foliage so that any ordinary errand at the upper level could have this exotic interlude. It was next to the Illustration department, and was run by John Norris Wood, who lived in Great Bardfield, was a lover of lizards, and who taught in Illustration. The route had hanging in it his drawings of iguanas draped over radiators at home in Essex. Behind the greenhouse were two identical unmarked adjoining doors, one to the Fashion Professor Janey Ironside's office, and one to Robin Darwin's flat, where he would sometimes retire in the afternoon to "do a bit of painting", I seem to remember Sir Hugh saying. The lift didn't reach the top floor, so one was forced to take the stair for the final ascent, turning on the windowed half landing sticking out from the facade, overlooking the Gore, the Park and the Albert Memorial. This disposition and conjunction of spaces and uses on the upper levels, this functionalist planning for the purposes of distraction and intrigue, formed a mute pedagogical assembly, handily close to our Environmental Design studio just along the way.

The studio had a certain spatial division, on the window side sat those who Fanny Foxon called the Men, the students who wanted to be architects when they grew up, and on the other side the Boys, who wanted to be boys when they grew up. The great Ed Jones commanded those by the window, and I idled away among the others near the wall. It was a brilliant year on both sides, and a surprising number went on to realise their ambitions after leaving the College.

I think all the Birmingham boys were by the wall, Pip Horne, David Connor and Julian. His drawing board was about midway between the front and back. Quite early on I watched over his shoulder as he sorted out a plan that would have taken me at least a week, if I could have managed it at all. At one point, unprompted he pushed a door back into a recess and in so doing resolved a major space. It was like the film, popular back then, of the train going from Victoria Station to Brighton in four minutes. Maybe it took him four minutes. Apart from being astonished, which I tried not to show, it switched on something in my head that since then has never turned off.

Nearly a decade after this, we taught together at Kingston on the Interior Design course for two or three years. It gave us the chance to mesh our thinking; we could spend odd pockets of time during the day discussing our persistent preoccupation with the scope and limits of interior design, sniffing out and trying to match insights and definitions. He was a great teacher, prickly on occasions but having also a deep empathy with the students, especially those with eccentricities. We began by taking the new Third Year students on a field trip to Milan, with the primary purpose of seeing the work of Aldo Rossi, in particular the housing he had completed at Gallaratese in the northeastern suburb of the city. Rossi's influence was widespread in the 80s, as much from his writings as from his buildings. In particular he had argued for the change of emphasis from buildings being tied to specific functions as in established Modernist theory, and instead talked of their role in the city as "silent monuments", elements in the collective image of the city carried in the minds of its citizens. The buildings were in some way necessarily unchanging, but required to accommodate changing uses with the changing times. Here, it seemed to us was a theory of the built environment that could apply equally to interior design as it did to pure architecture, that is equally relevant to making new buildings and to intervening in the existing that is the historical role of interior design. Confirmation of this came not on the visit to the housing, but the next day when we went to the Romanesque church of Sant'Ambrogio. Within the church, sitting in bays on the aisles were a series of chapels inserted at different times, and consequently in different architectural styles. Never-the-less, because of a skilful correspondence between the existing and the new interventions, they could be read both separately and as a whole. Some time later, back at Kingston, walking down the alley on the way to the pub for lunch, he said there and then that all aspects of the subject could be grouped under one term, "stripping back", that a set of relationships could be set down, making something akin to a theory.

At some point, inevitably, he needed to give his attention to his practice. The great seminal project from that time is the Metropolis recording studios in Chiswick, that PTCO designed in the 80s. The conversion remains one of the best and most instructive of all works of intervention worldwide in the last 30 years. It is a full and fitting response to the initial crystallising inspiration we found that day in the old church in Milan.

FRED SCOTT   LONDON 11TH AUGUST, VILLESPASSANS 24TH JUNE 2014

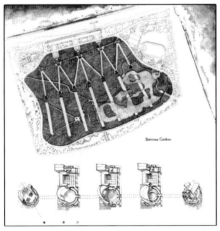

PROPOSAL FOR A NIGHT PARK AT BATTERSEA
FRED SCOTT WITH PTCO

RIVERSIDE
1997

We had designed this client's previous house back in the 1980s. It was a grand affair of around 10,000 square feet with a swimming pool and tennis court, extensive grounds, and live-in staff to help look after it all. The décor was traditional with antiques. However by now the family had grown up and left home. The house and upkeep had become too much. So we got a call asking us to meet at the house to analyse how the space was working. Our conclusion was that of the original space just 4,000 square feet was being used, and a new place of this size would provide a very comfortable downsize.

They had already decided they were ready to move back into central London and settled on a couple of neighbouring apartments in Riverside One, a block designed by Norman Foster and built in the 1980s on the Battersea bank of the river Thames. The apartments had been fitted out to a developer finish and by now felt a little tired, but the outlook was very special with amazing views of the river, old Chelsea embankment and Albert Bridge.

The atmosphere was dreamy, with the traffic on Cheyne Walk and riverboats gliding silently by, and the light off the river and the lights on the bridge at night providing all the visual stimulation necessary. Our clients were far from minimalists, and were wary of a stripped-back approach, however they agreed that a contemporary fit-out was appropriate. They embraced the idea of creating a cool sequence of interconnecting spaces that could either be opened up or shut down depending on privacy, mood and time of day. Whilst not having any exterior balconies, the apartment had floor to ceiling glass walls that were designed to open right up. There was a secondary glass balustrade to prevent a fall into the river below. The external elements were key in our design of the fit-out. The master bedroom was positioned to catch the sunrise and immense mirrored doors can be moved to play with the views.

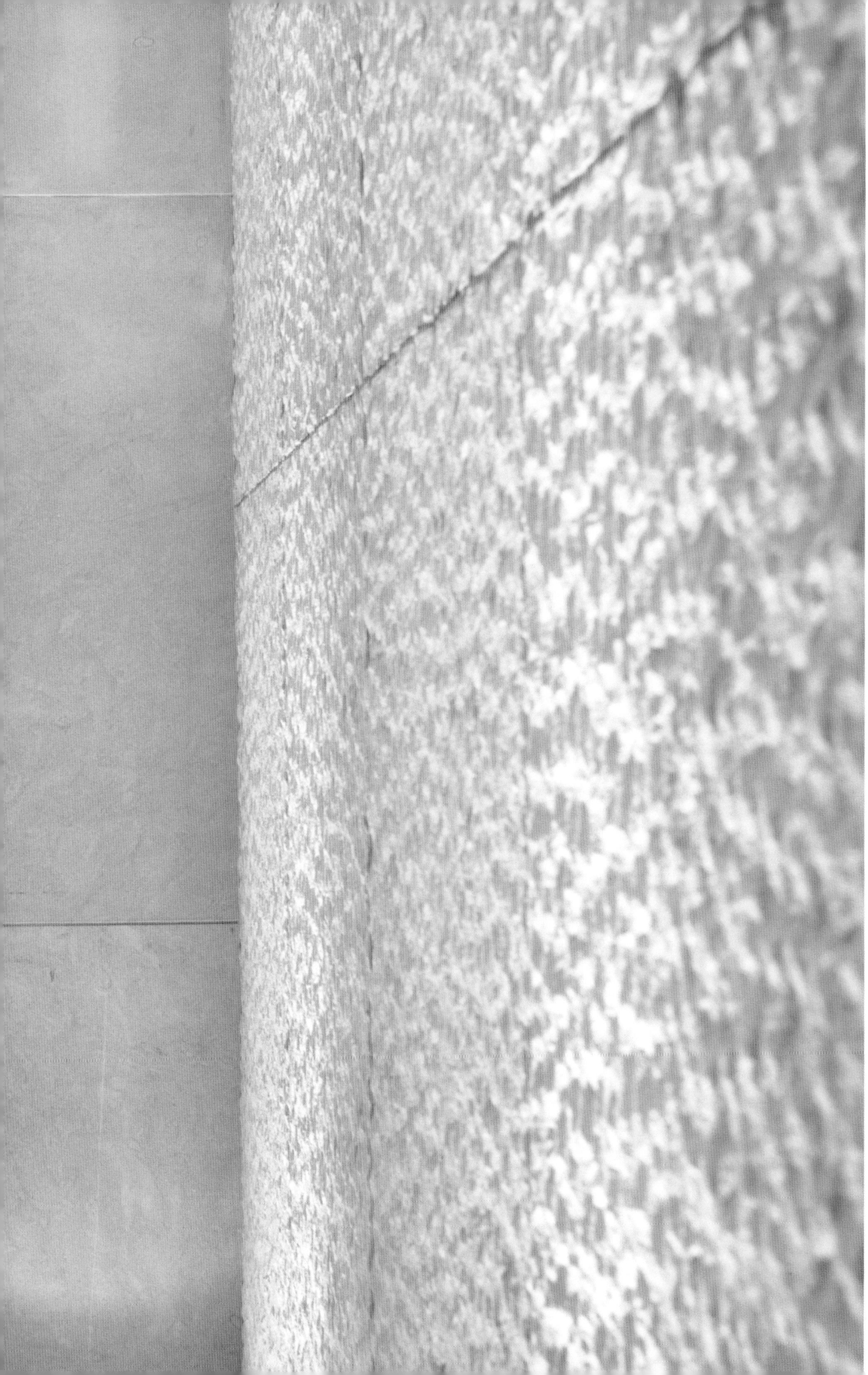

STAMFORD BROOK

STAMFORD BROOK
2001

When we first started out, back in the 1970s, we shared a studio in Fulham with two young property developers. Their particular interest then was to find so-called "backland" sites and convert them into interesting residential or commercial sites. These were generally old light industrial garages tucked in amongst residential streets. We helped them work on a number of these and so learned about the issues related to these developments. They were interesting design puzzles which also gave me my first valuable insight into building for oneself. A seed had been planted and, after years of searching, I stumbled across one such site that looked like it had potential.

The site was at Stamford Brook in West London. It was first built on in 1876 as stables for horses and living accommodation for a groom and his family. They worked for the London General Omnibus Company, a French owned company who by then had taken over the majority of the London horse-drawn omnibus companies. Post-1920s ownership moved to other transport related companies—removal contractors, motor haulage contractors, taxi services and finally a car bodywork repairer.

The original stables were still just discernable but the whole site had been roofed over and was filled with cars and car body parts. The tenant was tied into a rather onerous lease and welcomed the possibility of release so he could move his company to more suitable accommodation. We worked with him and an existing client to secure the site, on the understanding that when/if planning permission was granted the tenant would vacate.

Planning was a lengthy battle with Hammersmith and Fulham Council, whose main concern was the possible loss of employment in the Borough. Neighbours were understandably concerned about overlooking of their properties. One was also very worried about potential cooking smells from the new domestic kitchens, which were to replace the existing cellulose car spray workshops!

It took a full three years and several applications to win approval on appeal. The breakthrough came when we agreed to move the PTA studio to the site. At that time our studio was in Chiswick, and by moving it to the borough of Hammersmith and Fulham we could demonstrate that there would actually be more local employment when the development was completed.

The planning permission was granted for two live/work units. The PT family was to live in one, with PTA in occupation of the studio alongside. A client who had funded the purchase of the site, was to own the other unit. We demolished all existing buildings and roof structures leaving only the original 4m high perimeter wall. This was cleaned, pointed, and strengthened, and became a key feature of the design.

The design concept was again about space, rather than building form. The idea was to create three courtyards that responded to layers of privacy into the site. The first dealt with cars, deliveries and access to the office, the second was a communal garden with access to both houses, and the third was a private garden space. With the high perimeter wall and a requirement to minimise overlooking, these internal courtyards along other inserted light-wells were invaluable.

The other key strategy, very much a PTA trademark, is the use of daylight from above, washing walls and stairs with light from glazing set into the roof.

The buildings were constructed with a concrete frame. This was to accommodate the basement structure

62

under one of the houses and to ensure that we only had one subcontractor on the site at the early stages. The frame also could deal with the large spans, as some of the spaces were industrial in proportion. We wanted the building to have all the advantages of lateral space, not normally associated with a typical London House, that people had recently discovered through 'Loft Living', but with all the practicalities of a house, with plenty of bedrooms, bathrooms, storage, car-parking and a green outlook.

The external walls are clad in used London Stock bricks. These were chosen to work with bricks that we had reclaimed during demolition. Originally the buildings had been constructed using bricks made locally and we wanted to continue this line.

During excavation of the concrete slab laid across the site, we uncovered the original granite setts that paved the stable yard. These were set aside for re-use. To lessen the impact of the large areas of glass and provide some screening both from the sun and from prying eyes, we devised moveable external slatted timber screens. These have become a bit of a trademark, and have since been widely copied. The windows themselves were framed in dark grey aluminium. At that time the choice available for metal-framed windows for domestic use was very limited. Now larger areas of glazing have become a more regular feature in new domestic architecture and finer systems are available.

We wanted to express the perimeter wall as it passed through the internal spaces, and so exposed brick became a key feature. We also used bare block-work and concrete floors. The higher roof spaces were cedar-joisted with birch ply as a finish between the joists. These were cost effective materials. The idea was to build a robust interior that would cope with large family life. The living space was at first floor. With the studio, it gave us vast lateral space and with access to an outside terrace and a sunny outlook over the communal middle courtyard. Everyone said it felt like a holiday house rather than a London house... 11 years on, when the kids had flown the nest, we were sad to leave.

STAMFORD BROOK

STAMFORD BROOK

DEEPWATER

DEEPWATER
2001–2002

Our client called this house Deepwater with a nod of respect to Frank Lloyd Wright's Fallingwater, his other favourite building. Like Fallingwater, Deepwater was constructed with water all around. The concrete basement was built within a raised water table, where the ground is saturated with constant running water. During construction of the underground structure the poor main contractor used to visit the site in the middle of each night to check on the de-watering pump. If this had failed the water pressure would have caused the partially completed structure to collapse.

Beneath this house, the second house sited within the Stamford Brook complex, there is now a majestic 14 metre long swimming pool. By over-sizing the basement beyond the above ground structure we were able to scoop light in and make the space bright and full of sunlight. It was the first big subterranean structure we had built and became the model for many other such developments, as in subsequent years the mania for below ground construction began to sweep across West London.

The original stable wall that surrounds the site protects the property and enables the house to become a tranquil oasis in the city. The ground floor opens out, by way of sliding glass screens, onto the courtyard gardens. The inside and outside is conceived as one space. Deep within the site it has complete calm and privacy. We hard-landscaped the garden with a rill and ponds so there are fish, the sound of water and from time to time a family of ducks... tiny lights are entwined within the evergreen jasmine. It is the perfect place to dine at night.

The first floor rises above the perimeter garden wall, so, to avoid any overlooking of neighbouring gardens beyond, we placed windows on this floor at both high and low levels. They either look up to the sky or down into the courtyards. Large glass skylights beam dramatic shafts of daylight into the house.

This floor is sumptuously spacious and light and the high north-facing window in the library studio is completely cosmic... an animated still life in which you can silently track a distant passing plane or gliding bird picked out against a northern sky.

There is an art in getting the balance right when building a new house... the balance between the architectural vision and a client's requests. It was enormously helpful that we had previously worked regularly with this client... we both understood and respected our contributions. The key is having a client's confidence, without which good work is impossible to achieve. We ask a client to list out what they want to achieve from a building, but get uncomfortable if they start including ideas about form or structure.

In this case the clients wanted to use a very pale limestone throughout the interior and took me to see their house in the South of France, which they had just finished using a similar material. Such a singular treatment unifies all the spaces, and cladding many of the walls in stone has given the building a timeless quality. It will be a brave person who tries to tamper with this one in the future. I love the idea of making parts of the interior hard to change. Buildings seem to have to pass a critical coming of age test when 20 years old. This is when they are most likely to be perceived to be dated and can become unappreciated. If they can survive this they become increasingly loved and respected. I am hopeful that Deepwater's interior will last as long as its structure.

The limestone was a pretty uniform material so, to add variation, we had it worked. It was polished, honed and, in key areas, grooved and chiselled to produce textures that reflected light in different ways. To add potency rougher textures were used where nakedness was most likely, at the poolside and in bathrooms.

The limestone was contrasted with two other key materials, American Walnut used for the upper floors, doors and joinery and Basalt or black granite, which we used for the ponds and rills in the landscape and in key walls both externally and internally. The walnut gives richness and warmth to the interior. The black basalt unites the overall composition from the outside to the inside. Again we are playing conceptual temporal games in which we ask what came first, the landscape, the building or the interior? Our client was very unsure about using the black basalt within the interior, but thankfully now they love it.

Jinny Blom worked with us on the external soft landscaping. The middle courtyard was finished in tumbled stone setts. Three multi-stem silver birch trees provide shade and tall grasses and allium flowers provide wispy colour and movement to contrast the solidity of the brickwork and masonry.

DEEPWATER

DEEPWATER

THE POWER OF TRUST

Julian paused and put his words carefully...

"I know you're not going to like this, but I want you to take a deep breath and trust me. I want to finish the central structural wall of Deepwater in this... " and handed me a sample of black granite. I took the suggested deep breath. Black walls were not what I had imagined for my home our friends know us as the "white people"). I went away to think about this carefully, before reacting. 15 years of close collaboration led up to this moment. Julian and I had worked together to build dozens of music studios, wrestling together over every detail of some beautifully crafted and unique spaces.

As a 12 year old I was first struck by the architectural bug, rifling furtively through my uncle's 1960s *Playboy* magazines (irresistible to a 12 year old). It's a tribute to Hugh Heffner's editorial team that what struck me was not the soon forgotten Playmate of the Month, but the plans for a Playboy Pad—designs for an apartment stretching across the whole penthouse floor of an imaginary Manhatten skyscraper. In beautifully finished architectural plans, the Pad featured stone floors in huge square slabs, a sunken conversation pit centred around a massive fireplace, and glass walls opening on to exterior terraces, all detailed with elegantly drawn trees. I was hooked. I soon graduated from top of my technical drawing class (where I learned how to draw pipe work beautifully with a free hand) to applying these skills to my own designs for imaginary houses.

This was the client that Julian inherited in 1984 after winning an architectural competition to design the Metropolis recording complex. Being young and naïve, I trudged around dozens of leading London architects, precociously interviewing some serious talent for my 'once in a lifetime' project. I had no idea who they were, beyond the work they showed me, and no preconceptions about who I was supposed to pick to show my fashionable good taste.

With hindsight, we had good judgment, and the competition included contributions from a talented and distinguished field including David Chipperfield, John Pawson and John McAslan, all at the early stages of their inspiring careers. Julian's contribution soared away from the pack. His fellow architects all produced designs centred around a central atrium with natural materials in well proportioned, symmetrical, straight lines. Their designs stood back respectfully from the building and evolved around the elegant proportions of a central atrium.

In contrast, Julian immediately understood that the studios could not be squeezed into rigid square boxes behind a linear facade. He delighted in the asymmetrical shapes required by the acoustics of the recording areas. The result was a dynamic irregular interior facade, bursting with life and energy. Instead of designing calm new build architecture, which just happened to be inside a 100 year old monumental building, Julian's scheme rejoiced in the freedom to push the boundaries of the old power station's interior. By doing so, he achieved something remarkable, which might never have secured planning permission had the facade had been open to public view from the street. Gangways and ramps soared through the space, and an adapted construction hoist lifted the heavy recording equipment in a free cage through the atrium.

So we set out on a life time's journey together. There is nothing an architect hates more than an inexperienced opinionated client who tries to tell him what to do. So when I came forwards with my own studio plans in hand, there was a quiet sigh from Julian's team. To his great credit, Julian soon understood that this was not because I wanted to take over as architect. This was rather the clearest way I could express my ideas developed from working in the worlds greatest recording studios. I also soon learned that I had come across a master of his art. I watched as Julian absorbed the technical aspects of my crude two-dimensional ideas, knocked them around, and evolved them into visionary spaces.

We made a pretty good job of it. First opened in 1989, after five years of intense design and build collaboration, Metropolis was a sensation in the recording world. It transformed the recording industry's attitude to design, light and environment. Built at the apex of the music industry, before the internet undermined revenue, it was the last of the great British recording complexes—a magnet to talented artists, producers and engineers. It remains to this day, substantially unchanged from Julian's original designs, still the centre of recording excellence in London.

So back to Julian's request that I trust him over the black granite wall. This was more than the usual banter between client and architect. He knew this would challenge me after 15 years working together. I also knew by then that Julian never ran away with his own agenda, but would listen carefully to my ideas and transform them beyond anything I could imagine. Julian in turn tolerated my ideas, and knew that I would only ask to change things if I had good reason. Both of us learned to listen carefully and to have faith in each other. Trust between client and architect has to be earned and flow both ways—it can only be built on deep mutual respect and is the vital foundation for a great building.

So my wife Chrissie and I talked it over, hated the idea, and decided to trust Julian anyway And of course we love it—the black granite wall is officially a triumph. Its flamed finish is tough, soft and velvety. It transforms the restrained palette of the house. And what a house! The 12 year old's dream pad has evolved through decades of shared building experience, and the hands of a master.

Deepwater wraps itself around us in an oasis of private tranquillity in the city. Unsuspecting taxi drivers and delivery men stop and wonder at its calm serenity—jolted out of their daily hustle into a moment's quiet reflection and admiration.

CAREY TAYLOR

'BLUE MOON' BY DOMINIC WELCH

CARAMEL
2004

It is shame that shops are becoming increasingly corporate and over-branded as this tends to exclude those that are architecturally crafted, that used to find an occasional place in the high street. Many well-known architects have cut their teeth designing memorable shops in London, and I hope that this tradition can be revived in the future. At PTA we enjoy undertaking these retail challenges and are generally asked to do so when our clients want something non-mainstream, with a sense of individuality and place.

Our client for this retail unit, which specialises in high quality children's clothing, asked us to work for her after visiting one of our new-build house projects. She liked the idea of presenting her clothes in an interior with a 'residential' feel. Our interpretation of this brief was to avoid making the shop overtly for children. Rather we chose to design it using a limited palette of materials and sense of space more generally associated with our residential projects, thus presenting the merchandise within a more domestic, 'life-style' environment.

We set up the main volume by simply hanging some dramatic plaster planes at high level—part ceiling, part wall. These contrasted with the tough concrete developer finish of the shell, which we left exposed behind the planes and along one high wall. Against this textural backdrop we designed a lightweight stainless steel and timber shelving and hanging system to display the clothes. This has a storage plinth at the base and back-lighting onto new/old brickwork behind. A long low elm reception counter containing a cash register and jewellery display sits in front of a freestanding white wall panel towards the front of the shop. To the rear of the space we have added a new window for extra daylight and here there is a diminutive space, with blackboard walls, for reading and drawing. The shop front included an over-scaled slatted timber door, like the front door of a house.

CARAMEL

CARAMEL

CARAMEL

OXFORD GARDENS

OXFORD GARDENS
2006–2007

Much of the work of the practice is involved with remodelling London houses. It is therefore difficult to single out any job that particularly represents this aspect of our work. Each is interesting and challenging, and requires a light architectural touch. In this case the existing building was a double-fronted detached Victorian villa, one in a row of similar buildings, in a tree-lined street in fashionable West London.

When I first started out in practice with David Connor in the late 1970s and early 1980s, we shared a great studio space in Fulham with two young property developers. At that time they were buying large houses in this part of London and separating them into apartments. Now 30 years later, the area was back in vogue and the trend was being reversed. The property was in serious state of dilapidation. There were major structural problems at the rear, where part of the back elevation was breaking away from the sidewalls. Accommodation was in two separate sections, a 'maisonette' on the upper level and an apartment on the lower ground floor. The maisonette had not been modernised since the 1940s and was in a terrible state, but underneath it all it was clear that there was an essentially good house struggling to survive.

Our clients were an extended family who, excluding the main reception rooms, all wanted their own territory, so we conceived the house as follows: private parents area with bedroom, bathroom, dressing and sitting room on the Top Floor, young children's space with interconnecting bedrooms, a family bathroom and workspace on the First Floor, and the main Reception Rooms of Sitting Room, Kitchen, Dining and Study/Library on the Raised Ground Floor. The Lower Ground floor was the older children's zone with three bedrooms and bathrooms, kitchen and a family TV room and their own entrance. Finally in a new basement space created under the building our clients wanted a generous gym space, sauna shower and extra storage.

As with all these projects the initially strategic moves are of reduction rather than addition. Firstly the back of the building required demolition before starting there—construction works. The new basement floor below the Lower Ground floor was excavated and a new structure inserted. This also provided a new foundation for the reconstruction of the rear of the property, along with a new rear extension, which would attempt to maximise the house's connection to the modest rear garden. The original heights and spaces needed restoration, as did stone arches, windows and shutters, and staircase.

As always with this nature of work it's a question of how much of the new works are expressed in a contemporary style and how much as original. As a rule of thumb if we can restore the original features then we do, however new works should clearly look contemporary. However the rules tend to be 'interpreted' in their detailed manifestation. We chose to restore the original stair (and balusters) as we liked its gentle sweep, but we inserted glass landings to maximise the effect of light from new skylights in the roof. The stairs treads were a beautiful old hardened pine and we had new 'engineered' floors made with top 10mm layer of old pine to match this exactly. This was a new intervention that was heavily influenced by the original, rather than textbook restoration. It transformed, and gave great unity, to the house. For internal walls our strategy was that all new partitions should be detailed in a contemporary way. The original external walls were insulated and then finished in second hand brick slips. Window frames and shutters were restored and remade and left in unpainted wood. So both the nature and strategy of the alteration was expressed through the choice of finished materials. Parts of the building that appeared to be old had in fact been reworked to a modern day specification.

To create the grand master bedroom/sitting room on the top floor we re-structured the roof holding it up with two new oak trusses that were left exposed in the space. We used large new skylights to flood the floor and the stairwell with light. At the back of the house we added a two-storey lightweight extension intended to link and unite the Ground and Lower Ground floors to the gardens. Jinny Blom worked again with us on their layout and planting. The house has been sold since we carried out the works and the new owners have kindly given us permission to photograph it as it is today.

ALDERLEY COURT

ALDERLEY COURT
2006-2007

Alderley Court is a group of houses, a pretty typical 1960s speculative development. The type you see on the edges of many small semi-rural towns in the UK. They are pretty basic but at least have gardens and were not packed as closely together as many similar developments today. A plot on this development was certainly not the obvious choice for a new-build PTA house, but to our client, a product designer, it was just perfect.

He was living on his own, he needed a workshop in an efficient house, a base from which he could reach good cycling country... an unpretentious house in a practical setting, with neighbours, a community, and shops within walking distance. However he couldn't put up with the existing house on the site: it was poorly constructed, dark, spatially cramped and was simply not good enough... it had to go.

So we were asked to build a replacement house of better quality. I have always liked the idea of working with a simple house form. Here the way this form could be set into a sloped site made it an interesting proposition.

The plan was to rebuild, making spatial improvements on the original, but pretty much working within the volume of the former building, so we did not upset either the immediate neighbours or the planners.

The original house was built on a slope with the garage tucked under it on the roadside. By excavating the ground further after demolition we were able to increase the size of the new house without increasing its external volume. The new house needed to sit well with the neighbouring properties, without being flashy or pretentious... just well thought through.

ALDERLEY COURT

ALDERLEY COURT

The new ground floor level was re-invented as the main entrance to the house, with a large space to house a collection of beautiful bicycles and a design studio and workshop. We excavated the ground to allow full daylight into this space from the garden side. This level was designed so that, if needed in the future, it could easily be converted into extra bedrooms, as there was only one main bedroom on the floor above.

The main living accommodation is on the upper level. The idea was to split it up into four essential functions: work, sleep, eat and sit. From the first sketch these were sited from east to west to track the daily path of sun and to perfect their relationship with immediate landscape. The study has a horizontal window to keep an eye over the driveway, the road and the outside world. The main bedroom catches the morning sun and opens across a glass bridge to the garden.

The kitchen is bright throughout the day and opens onto a deck set into the garden. The living space is set up for the evening sun and has its own outside terrace with views towards the town. It is all very simple. Each space directly connects to the next. There is no circulation space, so it is extremely efficient.

Each room has a dramatic pitched ceiling up into the pitched roof. Two large central skylights set near the ridge of the roof wash the main stair and bathrooms with daylight from above. The floors are cast concrete slabs or wide Douglas Fir boards. The brickwork is made up of a mix of second hand red stock, which we have used both inside and outside the house. The joinery was all designed in with the house to make the simple spaces function well. Dan Pearson worked with us on the external landscaping.

The house may not look like an architectural masterpiece, but it is very special spatially. Our aim was to make it modest externally and spacious inside, the antithesis of the house it replaced. Our client says "It's like a gallery. Every room I look in and every space I see is special." Considering the modest site and surroundings this was quite an achievement.

ALDERLEY COURT

AVONDALE PARK

AVONDALE PARK
2009–2010

We enjoy the complexity of working with existing buildings, and I suspect we are generally biased towards trying to retain and evolve a structure when possible, but only if it can be successfully reworked as a complete architectural entity. This project was one where we tried to retain a building, but in the end used a sequence of planning applications to demonstrate and persuade others that, given the approved change of use to residential, a new building was a better solution.

A former Chapel of Rest stood on this site, which is within the curtilage of a well-used neighbourhood park on the edge of Notting Hill district in London. The chapel building looked quite imposing but its scale was deceptive, it was very small with a total floor plan of just 92 square metres. In recent years it had been rented out as a boxing club, with just one ring in the centre of the space. The club had moved on, and the local authority had chosen to sell the building. Our client was a design journalist and her young family. They lived nearby but wanted more space and thought the Chapel of Rest could be converted into something special.

Having established a change of use to residential, we developed two designs one that retained the existing building and one that proposed its demolition. The site was quite tight and had numerous restrictions from neighbouring properties. Our clients were not satisfied with the amount of achievable accommodation using the space that was available above ground and so underground development became a key factor. In this instance it would have been a complex task to try and retain the existing building and dig a basement. Of course we could have demolished and rebuilt the 'retained' part of the chapel, but a new-build 'converted' building was not an option we wanted to consider! Luckily the planners agreed and supported our application for a completely new design. To non-residents of the UK this may all seem like madness. We live on a small island. Here space for new buildings is hard to find and there are very strong lobbies to retain old buildings.

The new house sits behind the original railings to the park and, like the chapel before it is approached from the side. The ground floor is the main living space with an intercommunicating kitchen and reception area. Concealed behind a tall flush door there is a separate workroom. The ground floor has large glazed doors onto both the front and rear gardens. House and garden can be united completely. A dramatic void space rises over the living space to a galleried master bedroom suite above. It has an upper connecting opening that can be closed for privacy.

    The top floor has three bedrooms and a bathroom. The lower ground has a guest bedroom, bathroom and TV room. Daylight into the underground space is provided via large structural glass panels set flush with the ground floor and rear garden.

    This used to be a brick-making neighbourhood and there is an old brick kiln opposite the house. We wanted to work with a brick facade albeit carefully structured to achieve its lightness at ground level. As at Stamford Brook the challenging site and neighbouring conditions have informed the character of the building and the way we fill it with light.

AVONDALE PARK

AVONDALE PARK

A COLLEAGUE'S CONTRIBUTION

If I were to commission a new house for myself, I would ask JPT to design it, even though I am a designer myself and know many talented architects around the world. I would choose Julian, because I know that every aspect of the building would be inspired, and that it would be well thought out at every scale. The building would look good from space, and when you open a kitchen drawer there would be a beautiful place for the teaspoons. The house would have a serenity, it would be modest and understated. It would appear to be effortless, though it would, in fact, be the result of 40 years of thinking and experimentation. The house would harmonise with the landscape, exterior and interior would intertwine, rooms would flow from one space to the next, colours and the materials would blend. The ventilation would work quietly, the lighting would be subtle, and the house would be kept heated and cooled with the minimum of energy. A house like this is a very rare experience. It liberates you from the mundane, sets you free from the every day issues of living. It leaves you free to think, about the universe and death—and those teaspoons.

I first met JPT at the Royal College of Art in London in 1974, when we were both starting our postgraduate studies. Our first project at the RCA was to design a flat for Julie Christie, a conversion of a typical London house. Julian's project was radical, almost anti-design, but beautifully drawn in pencil and crayon and then the paper was coated in butter. He very generously later gave me these drawings and they still hang in my living room.

The Three House Project that he did for his final show at the RCA, was outstanding. It was a very theoretical project rooted in the landscape of the South Downs. The drawings were stunning, and that year won him the Royal College of Art Drawing Prize. Mind you, I won the Miss RCA contest, which was probably harder.

We later set up business in a cupboard (a small room) in the King's Road, Chelsea as designers, accepting whatever work came our way. I worked closely with Julian and later Gunner Orefelt for the next 12 years, building up the company.

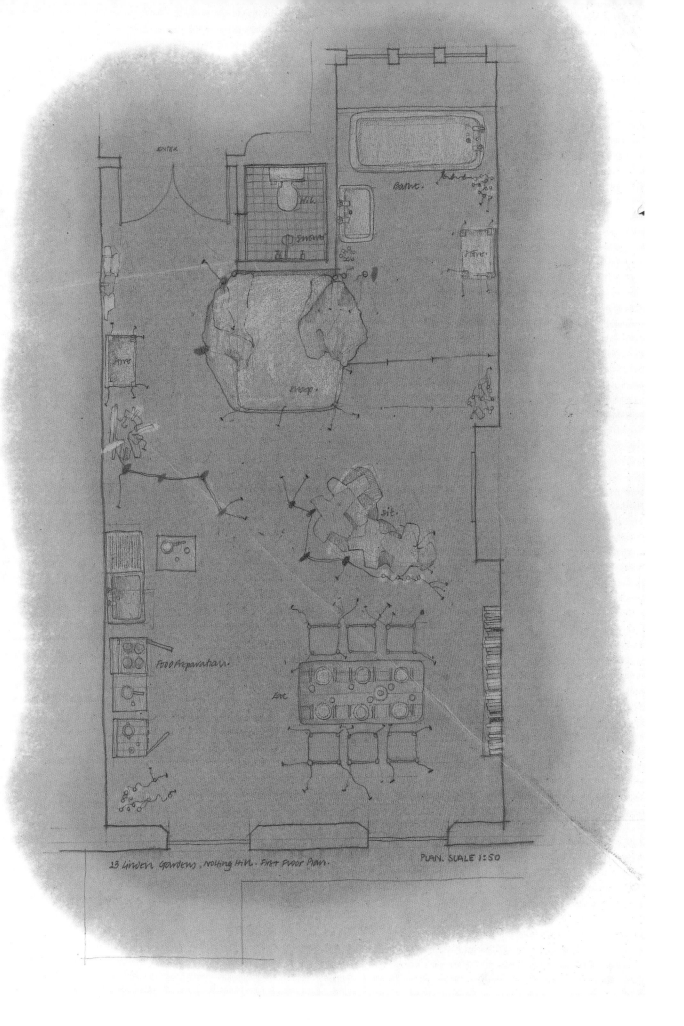

ENTER

W.C.

shower

BATH

BASIN

STOVE

prep.

sit.

Food Preparation.

eat.

23 Linden Gardens, Notting Hill. First Floor Plan.

PLAN. SCALE 1:50

THE SITTING AREA

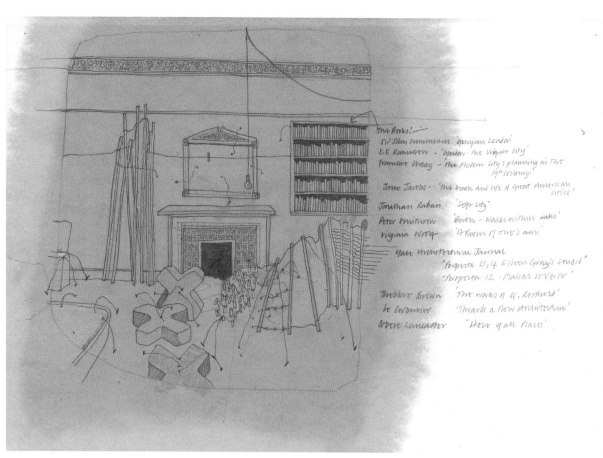

THE BOOKS:-

Sir John Summerson 'Georgian London'

S.E. Rasmussen - 'London the Unique City'

Francoise Choay - The Modern City: planning in the
19th century.

Jane Jacobs - 'The Death and Life of Great American
cities'

Jonathan Raban 'Soft City'

Peter Smithson 'Bath - Walks within Walls'

Virginia Woolf 'A Room of one's own'

Your Architectural Journal
"Perspecta 13/14 Eileen Gray's Studio"
"Perspecta 12 - Maison Jeverre"

Theodore Brown 'The works of G. Rietveld'

Le Corbusier 'Towards a New Architecture'

Osbert Lancaster "Here of all places"

Two early projects were flat renovations firstly for Adam Ant, the pop star, and next a flat for his guitarist Marco Pironi. I used long sticks in these interiors, smooth lacquered versions in Adam's flat and rougher ones in Marco's flat. These were not just ordinary sticks. They originated from Julian's earlier 3 Houses in a Landscape project. They were sticks to measure yourself in space and time. I liked them very much and they seemed to work: when in those interiors I never felt lost.

As the office grew it was Julian who kept the business running well, through the application of common sense, but he was always insistent that interesting design should take precedence over commercial considerations. His masterpiece from this era was Metropolis Recording Studios, an incredibly complex project, fitting a highly technical programme into an old defunct power station. This is construction at its most difficult, and yet he produced a result that is spectacular, functional but still very comfortable to inhabit.

What I respected in Julian was his thoroughness: he was very good at concepts, theory, structure, planning, detail, construction management, all of the social and technical skills that are needed to be a designer. What I admire most, however, is his exceptional artistry and creativity.

David Connor ARCHITECT/DESIGNER AND COLLEAGUE FROM THE PRE PTA YEARS

SENTRY

SENTRY
2011

I struggle when asked for my architectural influences. In spite of spending most of my life in London, I am drawn back to my Royal College project on landscape and man's early responses to his natural environment. At that time I was particularly keen on the symbolic landscape work of painters like Paul Nash and the moody photography of Fay Godwin. The British countryside is in my psyche. London is a cool, multi-cultural place to live and I love it, but I am sometimes frustrated by many Londoners' chauvinistic attitude to rural living.

At PTA we had done a few schemes for country houses but none had seen the light of day. So I decided to do something about that and spent a few years searching for a rural site for a new build house. There was an agenda. I wanted to attempt to show that contemporary houses could be designed to work with a special landscape and that houses designed to have a low environmental impact didn't need to look too 'alternative'.

After years of fruitless driving and searching I found the place, an old prefabricated bungalow with outbuildings set on the edge of a four acre, beautifully appointed, field in Dartmoor National Park. It also came with another four acres of sloped ancient woodland set amongst large megalithic granite outcrops. The site came with planning permission for a "futuristic" building nick-named locally the "one-eyed slug." Perfect!

The ideas started as usual with an outside space. In this instance it was a large terrace set over a slope between the woodland and meadow. This could be perfectly placed in the South -West corner of the plot, high in the canopy of the trees. It would provide some protected space beside the house, an outside 'room' where we could grow herbs, beyond which the landscape could be wild and natural. Below the terrace would be set the bulk of the house, the extra bit needed when family and friends came to stay.

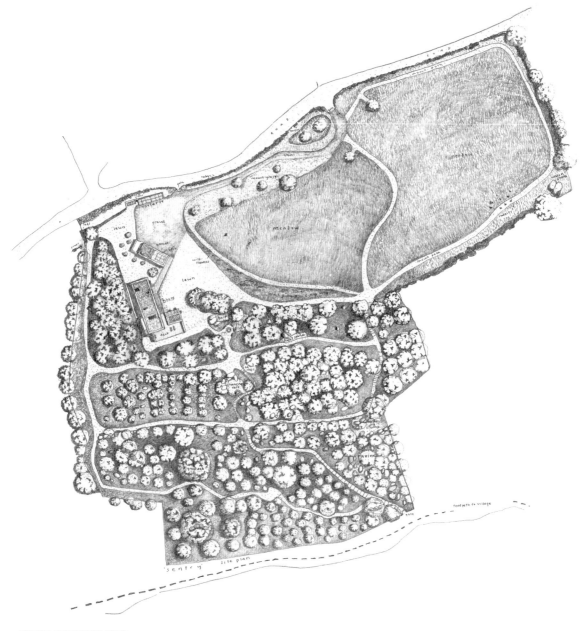

SENTRY LANDSCAPE DRAWING
JULIAN POWELL-TUCK

The next idea was an East–West oriented block, which hooked over the terrace, an inhabited wall at the edge of the meadow. Set on only one level it becomes a scale against which the changing natural contours of the ground can be measured and viewed. Into its plain stone facade large windows are cut. Each window is carefully set up with a distinctive view and relationship with the landscape. Finally a third block addresses the entrance drive and houses plant room, garage and studio workspace.

This was a simple diagram that we were determined not to embellish with added architectural devices or materials. It needed to have a primitive toughness to it like a fortification. I was also keen on the East–West orientation, which I have noticed is a characteristic of many early farmhouses.

There was no inherited garden and so the natural landscape could come right up to the house. The outside is built from granite, "tractored" down the narrow lanes from the local quarry. The roof is flat, highly insulated and covered with sedum and solar thermal panels. The walls are 700mm thick and also highly insulated. The sun rises and shines into the master bedroom and then warms the key living spaces throughout the day. Solar thermal panels on the roof and an air source heat pump provide the heating and a PV array generates electricity, so that incoming and outgoing energy costs achieve a balance.

We had lived with an open plan kitchen, dining and living space in our last house. This was fine with small children but as the family grew older our house needed to cater for differing as well as collective activities. We wanted to retain the lateral space that we were used to, but then provide some separation by making interconnecting spaces rather than rooms and corridors. Each room or space opens from another. The entrance is via a lobby straight into a large sitting room. This room most obviously then leads to the kitchen/dining room, and less obviously to a study and onto the master bedroom in the other direction. Both sitting room and kitchen have big sliding doors onto the terrace so that it all can be opened up for events.

The kitchen is the hub of the house where everyone comes together. From it a stair leads down to a family TV space, which in turn leads to four further bedrooms and bath/shower rooms and utility rooms. The plan is really very simple, but is one of the most successful aspects of the house. The house feels light and spacious, but also democratic in that people can find their own spaces too.

Inside, the house is minimally detailed with plastered walls painted in a pale tone; floors are oak or granite. The idea was to keep it simple as the view from each window was so special. We designed the fitted architectural joinery and Russell Pinch designed some of the key freestanding pieces of furniture. Each space opens from the next so that there is little circulation space and privacy is subliminal. The house works on one level when it's just us, but can open up to welcome friends and family when they want a break from real life in the city!

SENTRY

METROPOLIS STUDIOS

SITE PLAN

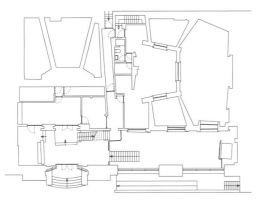

GROUND FLOOR PLAN

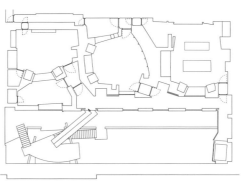

SECOND FLOOR PLAN

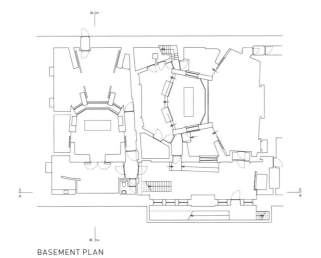

BASEMENT PLAN

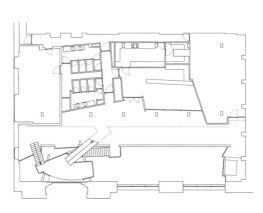

FIRST FLOOR PLAN

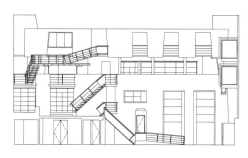

SECTION AA

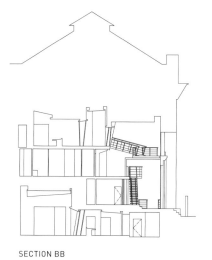

SECTION BB

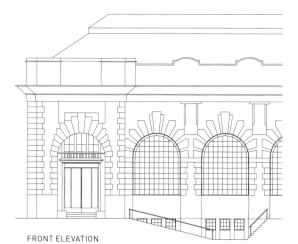

FRONT ELEVATION

LAMPTON PLACE

SECTION AA

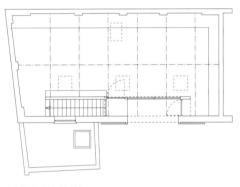

FIRST FLOOR PLAN

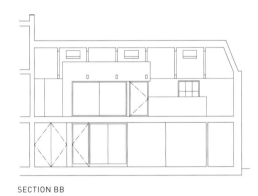

SECTION BB

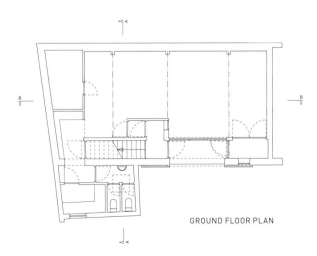

GROUND FLOOR PLAN

FRONT ELEVATION

M SALON

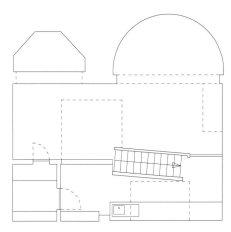

MEZZANINE LEVEL PLAN

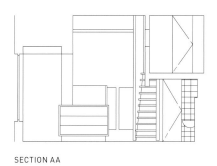

SECTION AA

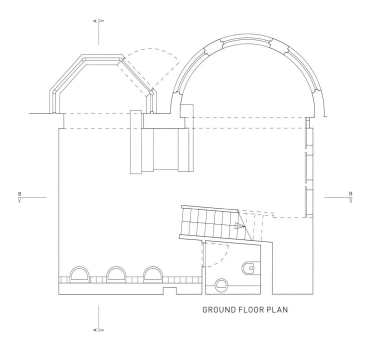

GROUND FLOOR PLAN

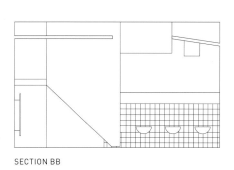

SECTION BB

RIVERSIDE

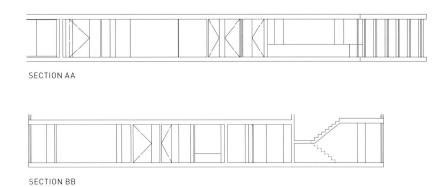

SECTION AA

SECTION BB

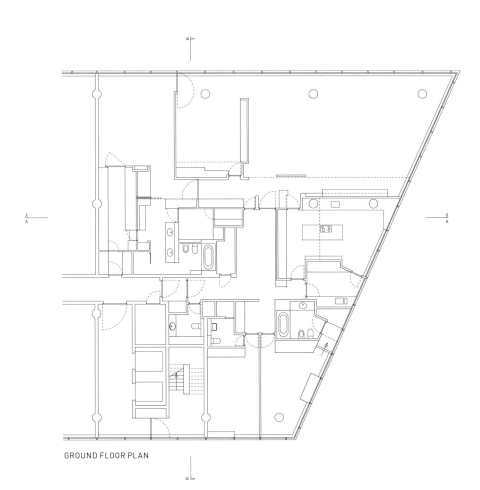

GROUND FLOOR PLAN

STAMFORD BROOK

SITE PLAN

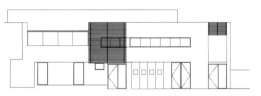

FRONT ELEVATION

SECTION AA

FIRST FLOOR PLAN

SECTION BB

GROUND FLOOR PLAN

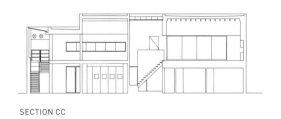

SECTION CC

DEEPWATER

SITE PLAN

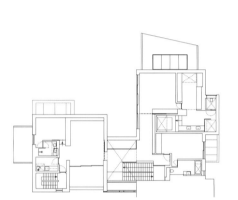

FIRST FLOOR PLAN

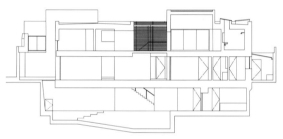

SECTION AA

GROUND FLOOR PLAN

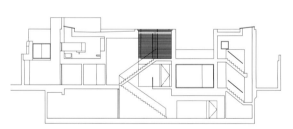

SECTION BB

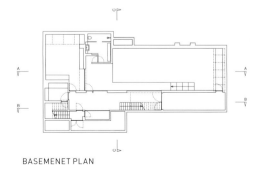

BASEMENET PLAN

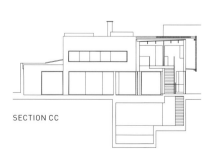

SECTION CC

200

CARAMEL

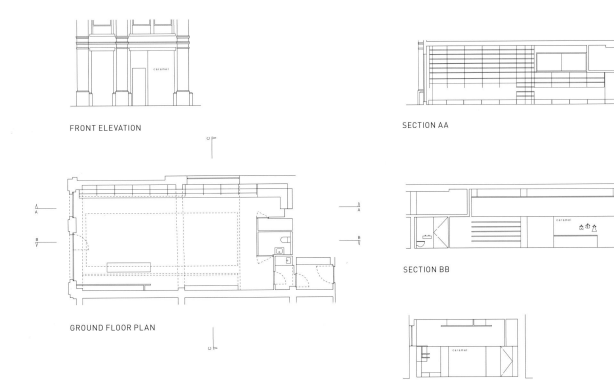

FRONT ELEVATION

SECTION AA

GROUND FLOOR PLAN

SECTION BB

SECTION CC

OXFORD GARDENS

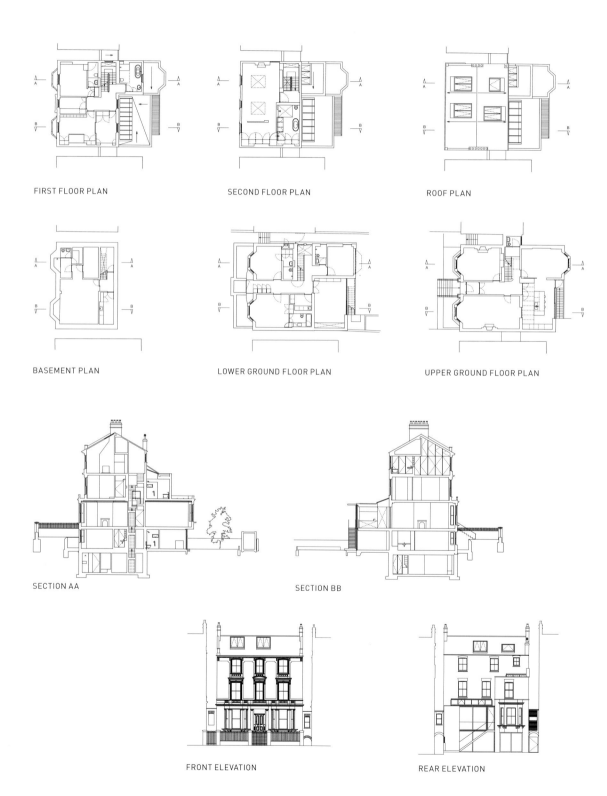

FIRST FLOOR PLAN

SECOND FLOOR PLAN

ROOF PLAN

BASEMENT PLAN

LOWER GROUND FLOOR PLAN

UPPER GROUND FLOOR PLAN

SECTION AA

SECTION BB

FRONT ELEVATION

REAR ELEVATION

ALDERLEY COURT

SITE PLAN

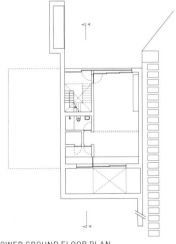

LOWER GROUND FLOOR PLAN

SECTION AA

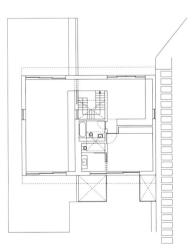

UPPER GROUND FLOOR PLAN

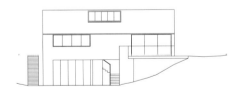

FRONT ELEVATION

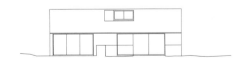

REAR ELEVATION

AVONDALE PARK

SITE PLAN

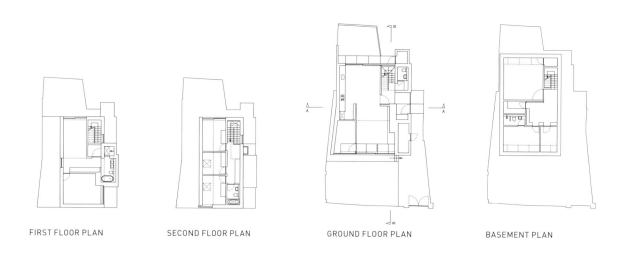

FIRST FLOOR PLAN   SECOND FLOOR PLAN   GROUND FLOOR PLAN   BASEMENT PLAN

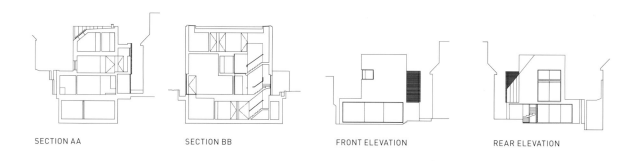

SECTION AA   SECTION BB   FRONT ELEVATION   REAR ELEVATION

SENTRY

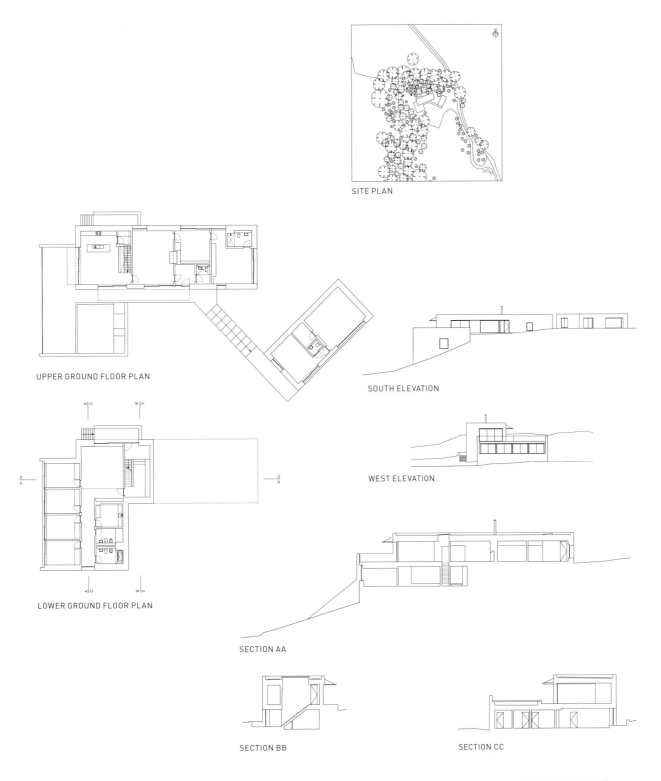

SITE PLAN

UPPER GROUND FLOOR PLAN

SOUTH ELEVATION

WEST ELEVATION

LOWER GROUND FLOOR PLAN

SECTION AA

SECTION BB

SECTION CC

ACKNOWLEDGMENTS

Powell Tuck Associates (PTA) was born out of the Powell Tuck Connor and Orefelt (PTCO) in 1990 and I would like to thank David Connor and Gunnar Orefelt for all the great times we had together. Timelines are somewhat blurred now but the first few phases of the Metropolis project were done by my team when we were all still at PTCO, and I know they will be pleased to see its inclusion in this book.

Two young members of my team at PTCO, Angus Shepherd and Adrian Lees were brave enough to join me in the new venture and for 20 years worked with me through thick and thin. I would like to thank them for all their support creativity, hard work and resolve, and I wish them all the very best in taking the practice forward in the next 20 years.

I would like to thank my good friend Michael Hodgson. We were at college together in the 1970s and although he has lived in California most of his life we have kept in touch. Along with the friendship there has always been a mutual admiration for our work. We have worked with him on a couple of projects in California and I was so pleased when he agreed to design this book.

Fred Scott and Carey Taylor also need a special mention for their enthusiasm and support over the years and for kindly agreeing to make their written contributions.

Then there is the extended team of architects and designers who worked at PTA and have played an enormous role in a portfolio of work, much of which is not included in this selection. On the opposite page is a list of PTA people and I wish to thank them all for their varying roles in delivering the projects.

JULIAN POWELL-TUCK, AUGUST 2014

PTA ARCHITECTS/DESIGNERS

Steve Appleby

Martina Caplazi

Katy Carter

Rajan D Chaudhary

Salvatore Contaldo

Lesley Cotton

Ian David

Thomas Denhof

Pete Dixon

Lorna Edwards

Rob Excell

Amy Ge

Steve Gittner

Andrew Gollifer (PTCO)

Grenville Herrald

Irene Iacolino

Sonya Jarvie

Adrian Lees

Gordon Leney

Yi-Hwa Lin

Vincent Westbrook

Craig Watson

Phillip Harrison

Hugh Mackay

Camille Mandy

Rita Mazeda

Simone McEwan

Peter Mance

Elisa Mondragon

Luigi Montefusco

Matt Moorhouse

Peter Murray (PTCO)

Susanna Mussotter

Julian Powell-Tuck

Gerard Rainey

Caroline Robertson

Nadia Salamo

Angus Shepherd

Bryony Smeed

Suzanne Smeeth

Annette Strauss

Mark Taylor

Jennifer Valone

Sehnaz Yilmaz

COPYRIGHT, PHOTO CREDITS

Artifice books on architecture
10A Acton Street
London
WC1X 9NG

T. +44 (0)207 713 5097
F. +44 (0)207 713 8682
sales@artificebooksonline.com
www.artificebooksonline.com

All opinions expressed within this publication are those of the authors and not necessarily of the publisher.

British Library Cataloguing-in-Publication Data. A CIP record for this book is available from the British Library.

ISBN 978 1 908967 49 7

Designed by Ph.D, A Design Office www.phdla.com

Photography of the Front Cover, pages 18, 59, and 64–65 by Julian Powell-Tuck

Photography of Metropolis, pages 2–4, and 78–83 by Richard Davies

Photography of Lambton Place and M Salon by Dennis Gillbert

Photography of Riverside by Henry Bourne

Photography of pages 56–57, and 99 by Carey Taylor

Photography of Oxford Gardens, pages 12, 72–75, 77, and 84–95 by James Merrell

Photography of Alderley Court and pages 9–10 by Simon Collins

Photography of Avondale Park, pages 5–6 by Leigh Simpson

Photography of Caramel and Sentry, pages 7–8, 11, 60–63, and 66–71 by Edmund Sumner

Every effort has been made to trace the copyright holders, but if any have been inadvertently overlooked the necessary arrangements will be made at the first opportunity.

Artifice books on architecture is an environmentally responsible company. After Metropolis, The Architecture and Design of Powell Tuck Associates is printed on sustainably sourced paper.